Start an Online Business

A No-Nonsense, No Hype How-To Guide to Help You Pick Your Online Business Model and Get Started Making Money Online

Jeff Gilder

ISBN: 978-1-7974-3875-7.

CONTENTS

INTRODUCTION

Congratulations on purchasing *Start an Online Business: A No-Nonsense, No Hype How-To Guide to Help You Pick Your Online Business Model and Get Started Making Money Online* and thank you for doing so!

We will give you a realistic and no nonsense explanation of how you can start and grow an online business in any field. We will not teach you to make millions overnight or make money without any work, but we will help you take the most important step - the first one. An unknown wise person once said, 'The dream is free, but the hustle is sold separately."

The road to becoming a business owner is not easy. For many who want to embark upon the online business owner lifestyle, they have no problem thinking about their lofty goals of success and fortune. Yet, in order to reach their goals, they have to put in the work, or the hustle. This book is designed to give you the true scoop on what you need to do in order to start your own online business.

As a word of caution, the information provided can

feel overwhelming, but it is important to note that by the time you finish, you will have everything you need to do to start your online business. Just take everything step-by-step, and you will be moving towards your goals in no time. Be mindful that there are lots of things that you may have to do on your own. There are lots of things to research. (Remember, it takes hard work.) The more you research in the more you connect with people who are doing what you want to do, the easier your journey will be. Always be open to learning more because you have to be adaptable as a business owner if you're going to be successful. There is no way around it. However, if you are determined to succeed, you will be able to overcome all the challenges that you will face. Stay positive and keep going. Keep your expectations manageable and take it baby step by baby step. Think of failure and setbacks as a positive thing. You will only know what works once you fail. So, fail a lot and learn a lot. You won't make a million overnight, but eventually you might.

If you do or if you don't, you've done the most important thing which is to take the first step.

This book will cover the mindset, tools and resources you need in order to be successful. In Chapter 1, the mindset of what makes a business owner successful will be examined. There are four key pillars one must have in order to make it in the online business world, and this chapter will make sure that you have them. The heart of the book is in Chapter 2. It explores 10 different business models that you can choose from to get started in the online business world. The info given is no fluff, concise, and informative. It highlights everything you need to know to start a particular online business. After reading about 10 different business models, Chapter 3 helps you figure out which model is the best choice for you. It also highlights the bones you will need in order to make your business successful. Chapter 4 highlights what success means for you and your business. It also helps you figure out how to scale your business and get more comfortable with the realities of being a business owner by outsourcing tasks that don't make a lot of money. The final chapter, Chapter 5, offers important considerations you should have when you are starting your business. Overall, the information in this book gives you a firm grasp of what you need to know before you begin your online business. Be sure to take notes and highlight your favorite portions so you can re-visit them at any time.

There's no need to spend a lot of money on expensive courses before even starting when you already have the necessary tools to start. The time to own your business is now. Keep reading to find out how you can take this step!

There are plenty of books on this subject on the market. Thanks again for choosing this one! Every effort was made to ensure it is full of as much useful information as   possible.   Please   enjoy!

CHAPTER 1: THE MINDSET OF A BUSINESS OWNER

Why would somebody want to leave the comfortable life of working a regular, stable, nine-to-five job and embark upon the unstable, wild world of owning your own online business? Well... there are many reasons.

The thrill of being your own boss is the first one. Many people love to do what they want to do when they want to do it. When you are your own boss, you do not have to worry about others telling you what to do. You are the one that gets to tell others what to do, and they HAVE to listen to you. When you are a business owner, you have the joy of being able to take what you see in your mind and make it become reality.

Moreover, having an online business helps you to be location independent and this is another reason why many people want their own online business. An online business is one you can do anywhere as long as you have a computer and internet connection. Many people are utilizing online business to see the world and live the life they've always dreamed about.

Another major reason becoming a business owner is attractive is because you are paid what you are worth. If you were working a traditional job, you would be paid an hourly rate, oftentimes, wishing that you were making more money. However, the amount of money you can make from owning your own business is astronomically higher than you can make by working for someone else. The work to pay ratio when you are a business owner is definitely better. In fact that ratio can be limitless, especially if your online business becomes successful. When you own your own business, someone does not become rich off your hard work. When you have your own business, you do not have to dread going to work every day, knowing that someone else is living a comfortable lifestyle because of your hard work.

As a business owner, you, and only you are the beneficiary of all the work you put in. You determine who to work with, whether they are employees or freelancers, because you are in charge. If you want to cut everyone's pay, you can. If you want to give everyone a raise, you can. You are the boss and what you say GOES. This is one of the most important reasons – you get to do what you want to do! This book will help you begin the journey towards owning your own business and becoming the online business owner you are destined to be.

Sure, having your own business sounds good, but those who want to be successful must have a certain mindset. Without it, you won't be able to make it. The basic mindset of a successful online business owner consists of four major pillars:

1.   **The first pillar** is that you must be committed to hard work. Some may even call you a workaholic and rightfully so. Business owners will put as much time as they need into their business. Successful business owners put in a lot of work. Sometimes, they put in a lot of work before they even see results. This is not normal for most people. Some people are afraid of hard work. They are

always looking for the shortcuts in life to do the least amount of work possible. Business owners do the exact opposite. They understand that hard work is necessary to achieve their dreams. They approach their journey to business ownership with the expectation that they are going to work hard. The hard work does not deter them, but rather the ability to not reach their dreams is more important than hard work. It's this obsessive commitment to hard work that drives business owners, and it is at the core of being one.

2.   **The second pillar** of the business owner's mindset is the willingness to invest money in their business. Business owners know that to make a business run, you have to invest money. Oftentimes, with limited resources, they find themselves investing their own money. They know how to save their money to help them make it through lean times. They have the discipline to put their profits back into their business instead of spending it. The money that they make, they use it to work for them. They are quick to learn and use the info to make more money.

On the other hand, investing money in their business can also be a business owner's downfall. If a business owner is investing too much money into a sinking ship, they are not being smart. However, successful business owners know when it's smart to stop investing in their money, but they are not afraid to spend it. Even if they spend too much money into their business, they are able to quickly make adjustments in the best interest of their business.

3.   **The third important pillar** of being a business owner is to know how to focus their time wisely. Working hard is important, but if you work hard on things that do not matter to your business, then your all your work is null and void. Successful business owners know how to focus

on the most important activities that help their businesses grow. They focus on the task that brings in money and outsource the rest. (More information about outsourcing will be given later in the book.) Once they figure out what activities make the most money for their business, they spend all their time on those tasks.

Successful business owners are master time management practitioners. It's easy to get sucked into the vortex of trying to do everything for your business. Successful business owners do the opposite. They focus on the most important things so they can have a well-rounded lifestyle. This commitment to focus and managing their time allows them to stay on the business path longer than those business owners who try to do everything and find them being burned out.

4.   **The fourth and final pillar** that successful business owners must have is the ability to be objective. Most people have a bias when it comes to their own abilities and efforts. These biases enable them to make bad decision after bad decision, especially when it comes to their business babies. Business owners are objective about their expectations and goals when it comes to their business. They are able to see if what they're doing is working or not and don't get emotional about it. They can handle feedback constructively, but they are their own most constructive critic. They take the feelings out of their business decisions and look at the data to see if it supports what they are trying to accomplish. If what they see supports their expectations and goals, then they continue to do those actions. However, if their expectations and goals are not being met, business owners do not feel bad about taking a new path to reach those goals or modifying their expectations and facing the reality. Unfortunately, many people have certain expectations about their business, but once they start working, they realize that

those expectations don't correlate to the real world. People love to think about business but are shocked what happens when they actually try to do business.

Business owners are not so committed to their ideas that they are not able to change. They understand that business is constantly changing, and they don't take these changes personally. This ability to be objective helps them to find the proper resources that will help their business succeed. If they feel they are too close to their own business, they don't mind asking mentors or hiring business coaches to given objective evaluation. Successful business owners know that being objective is the only way that their business can survive, and they seek out best information to help them measure their business against so they can survive long-term.

In conclusion, being a business owner is a dream that many have, but not many are willing to work to archive it. Having a successful business is not just selling your company for millions of bucks. Having a successful business means a commitment to excellence and lots of hard work reeling to meet your business's goals and expectations. In order to be a true business owner, you must have a foundation consisting these four pillars. The first is a love for hard work; the second is a commitment to investing money in your business; business; the third is knowing how to focus on the money making task of your business and the fourth pillar is knowing how to be objective.

Business ownership is very rewarding but there is hard work that goes into it. If you are willing to make the commitment, then you're going to have a lot of fun. If you're not sold on the hard work that it takes to be successful, then stop reading now. However, if you're up to the challenge, keep reading. In Chapter 2, we will explore different types of online business models, and the fun will really begin.

CHAPTER 2: EXAMINING DIFFERENT ONLINE BUSINESS MODELS

Thanks to technology and an increasingly global workforce, there are lots of different ways you can make money online. Before you decide which business to start with, it's important to first understand the different business models that are available. This chapter will explore different online business models you can choose from. Each business model will explain what the business model is and how you can make money with the business model; the types of skills and time and monetary investment you need to get start; how long it will take to get started; guide of quick steps; pros and cons of the business model; and a section that offers why people fail with the business model that is noted. The business models will be divided into three different sections: retail, freelancing, and influencer and affiliate marketing.

Let's begin!

☐

Online Retail Business Models

All the businesses in this section deal with how to use the retail business model in an online setting. The ideas in this section can be done whether you have money for startup costs or even if you don't. It also highlights some of the most important things to keep in mind if you decide to use one of these online business models.

Dropshipping

Intro

Dropshipping is an online business model that does not require you to have any upfront inventory. Dropshipping is a simple process. You research products to decide what you want to dropship. Once you decide what you want to sell, you find a company that does dropshipping for that particular product. When you decide what you to sell, look at the company's prices and add your profit to the price. The total price will be the price that your customers pay you. After determining the price, you then create a website or ad and drive customers to the website with the ad. Once the customer places the order on your website, you then go back to the site that dropships the product and place the customer's order there. You pay the cost and pocket the profit. The dropshipping company then sends out the products to your customer from their warehouse so you don't have to deal with the product at all. With just using a few clicks of a button, you get to keep the profit without the hassle of dealing with inventory or fulfilling orders.

Skills and Money Investment

Research Skills -Research skills are a must for this

business model. You have to be willing to find dropshippers that dropship the product you want. Then you want to check out the reviews of the company to see if other companies have had experiences with the company. Once you find the company you want to work, then you are ready to take action.

Writing Skills - You also need to have writing skills for this business model. You'll need to be able to write copy on your website to describe what the product is. You also need to know how to write advertisements.

Keyword and SEO Research Skills - When people type phrases into the Google search bar, they are using keywords. Knowing how to find those keywords and use them to your advantage is at the heart of keyword research skills. Entering words into Google that your potential customers may use helps you see if the product you want to sell is something that people want to buy. Knowing that you have keywords that people are searching for will help you be successful. A great place to look for keywords is using the Google Keyword Planner, which is a free tool.

SEO stands for search engine optimization and these skills help you get your website on the first page of Google. Knowing how to properly use SEO can help you bring in more sales. There're certain places you can add keywords to give your website a boost. If you do not have SEO skills now, it is not a deal-breaker. You can slowly learn and optimize your website later.

Monetary Investment - $0 - $100

For the monetary investment, you don't need a lot of money. You can either use a website that is already up like Shopify or BigCartel, or you can create your own website and domain name for a few bucks.

How Long Does It Take To Start – Immediately - A few days

This business model does not require a lot of time to start up. You can spend four hours researching, or maybe less, to find a product that you want to drop ship. Once you figure out your product, you can set up your site, create a few ads, and you'll be ready to go.

What to Do to Get Started

1.   Research the product that you want to dropship. Find a product and make sure that the company is reputable and has great reviews about the quality of the product.

2.   Create your website. Make sure your pictures look great. Some companies allow you to use the same pictures from there site. Others require that you use your own pictures of your websites. If this information is not clearly listed, you can ask the dropshipping company what their policy is about this. One of the best website creators to start is using Big Cartel or Shopify.

3.   Be sure to have an email collector like AWeber or MailChimp so you can collect your customers' emails. You can offer a discount in exchange for your customers' emails. Once you have their emails, you can always advertise them. This step is simple to do by adding a few lines of code to your website.

4.   Create an advertisement for your business and post it where customers can see it. You can use Facebook, YouTube, or other social media platforms to begin. Don't be afraid to tap into your current network of family and friends to get your first sales.

5.   Once you make your sales, you can invest in more advertising to promote your company more.

Pros and Cons

Pros

The pros of this business are that it does not cost a lot of money to start. You can utilize free tools so that you don't have to spend any money on websites or hosting.

Another pro of this type of business model is that you don't have to have a lot of money to get started. Since you don't have to have any inventory, you can quickly set up a website and focus on acquiring customers, which is the lifeline of any business. The key to any business is getting your first customer as soon as possible, and then using the steps you used to get that first customer to get more customers.

This business model is great for people who have a lot of time but not a lot of money as a way to make money. Once they make money, they can use the profits to invest back into the business.

If you want to focus on print on demand items, like books or t-shirts or any other pain under my company's, you may need to have additional skills such as graphic designing or writing. Popular print-on-demand websites include teespring.com, Zazzle, and printful.com.

Cons

Choosing the right product to sell is very important when trying to decide what you want to sell. In order to be successful, you have to make sales. If you choose a very competitive niche, it can take a while in order to sell products. Therefore, you want to make sure your branding is different from other companies to set yourself apart from your competitors.

If you decide to jump right into paid advertising, you may lose money if you aren't able to make customers quickly. If you are cash-strapped, you should rely more on word-of-mouth advertising to make a few sales, and then use that money to invest in paid advertising.

Why People Fail

People fail with dropshipping because they give up too soon, and don't adjust their marketing strategies fast enough. If you're in a competitive niche, you may want to give yourself a week or two to see if any sales come in. If none come in, then adjust your strategy.

E-Commerce

Intro

Similar to drop shipping, the e-commerce business model sells products. Instead of focusing on working with companies that dropship items, you focus on any product that you want to sell. You are in charge of handling the storing of the inventory and fulfilling the orders or packing them for sale with this model.

Skills and Money Investment

Research Skills -Research skills are important for this business, but because you are selling what you want to, you don't have to worry about looking for dropshipping companies. Research is more important for looking at other people who are selling what you're selling to see how you can differentiate your business from them.

Writing Skills - You also need to have writing skills for this business model. Knowing how to write product descriptions and advertisement is very helpful.

SEO and Keyword Research Skills – Both are valuable to give your site an extra boost so you can be successful.

Monetary Investment -$0 - $1000+

The monetary investment for this business model is more involved. You will need to have capital in order to buy products. If you are not able to store the products at your house, you may need to find somewhere to house your products.

Additionally, if you are going to be shipping things for yourself, you may have to hire extra help to help you ship. The cheap option is to hire a young person or see if a young person will 'intern' at your company to help you ship it. The more expensive option is to hire help. This way, help will be more reliable. However, you may not be able to hire people until you make enough sales that demonstrate you need more help.

The next cost you need to consider is how to store your products. The cheap option is to house the products at your house. The more expensive is finding storage or buying extra storage at your house, such as a shed. Another option that costs, but makes more sense, will be to look into fulfillment companies where you can ship products to the company and they will fulfill and ship the orders out for you. More will be talked about in the Amazon FBA model for this.

The next monetary investment with this business model you may want to consider is hiring customer service help. Most e-commerce companies live and die by how good their customer service is. Having great customer service experience really helps your company stand out. On the cheaper end, you can look into a ticket system like Freshdesk which is free that allows you to send out canned responses, or you can hire someone for customer service help.

How Long Does It Take To Start - A few days to weeks

How fast you can start depends on how soon you start your website and how fast you can get your capital to buy your products. What you are selling will determine how long it to get started. If you are selling artwork, you can sell on the website as soon as you finish a painting. If you need capital up front, you will have to wait until you get the capital in order to start.

What to Do to Get Started

1. Research the product that you want to sell. Be sure to look at other competitors to make sure that they are not selling in the same way that you want to sell. You also want to check the quality of the product that you want to sell to see if that's what's going to set you apart.

2. Create your website. Make sure your pictures look great. You can either create your own or you can leverage a website like Amazon, Etsy, or eBay to get started. Once you get a little more capital, you can then create your own website to draw in customers if you like. Just be aware that sites like Amazon, Etsy, or eBay, may charge you to list on their website so you would have to weigh the benefits based on your budget.

3. Be sure to have an email collector like Aweber or MailChimp so you can collect your customers' emails. You can offer a discount in exchange for your customers' emails. Once you have their emails, you can always advertise them. This step is simple to do by adding a few

lines of code to your website.

4.   Create an advertisement for your business and start putting the ad everywhere that you can.

5.   When someone buys from you, be sure to ship their product out in a timely fashion. You also will want to make sure to have your shipping and returns policy clearly listed to avoid any confusion.

Pros and Cons

Pros

The first pro for this business is that you are not limited to which companies that offer dropshipping. You have more freedom in determining what you want to sell.

The next pro is that you have the potential to make a lot more money if you can buy more items in bulk. You may be able to get those items from the manufacturer at a lower price which translates to higher profits from you.

Cons

This process is a lot more involved. You have to first figure out if you have the capital and if you're going to purchase a lot of items in bulk, you have to make sure that you can sell them. You don't want to be stuck with the extra product.

You also have to deal with customers now. Instead of having another company deal with your customer service, you have to handle that on your own. Shipping is another concern that you must have with this type of business. You have to have policies in place to help you deal with loss products and any other gripes customers may have.

The cost to start is a lot higher than other businesses; thus, initially, you may not have as much money to put into advertising which could take you longer in order to get the first sell. As soon as you get your first customer, you can figure out how much it will cost you to acquire a customer and use that knowledge to get more clients.

Why People Fail

People fail with e-commerce because they spend too much money on their capital, and they can't get rid of it. Keeping your costs low is the key to surviving this online business model. If you can figure out what works on a limited budget, you can figure out what works when you get more money.

Amazon FBA

Intro

This business model is a combination of drop shipping and e-commerce, except it takes both of these models, combines them, and takes them to the next level. This model leverages Amazon to ship items that you want to sell. You are in charge of finding the product that you want to sell, either by buying it in bulk or getting it manufactured. Once you get your products in bulk, you then have to ship it to an Amazon warehouse and then Amazon handles the shipping process. You then can help market the products to make sure that it sells. Once it sells, you start the process all over again.

Skills and Monetary Investment

Research Skills -Research skills are a must for this business model. You have to find the best products to get manufactured that will help you make the most money. Not only the best products, but you have to find the best products at the best price. Don't skimp on this step.

Writing Skills - You don't have to worry about writing descriptions on your own website, but you still need to write eye-catching descriptions on Amazon's website. If you are going to also use your own advertisements, you must have some sense of writing copy is Will.

Monetary Investment - $0 - $1000+

This business model requires much more in upfront capital. Some of the initial costs are signing up for an Amazon Seller's Account. After identifying the manufacturer or your product, you will most likely spend thousands in capital. If you are getting the items manufactured overseas, then you will need to also include shipping cost back to the US or to the nearest Amazon facility. Once the inventory gets to the Amazon facility, you will have to pay warehouse and fulfillment costs. Amazon will charge you based on how much space your inventory takes up in your warehouse and per item that they fulfill and ship for you. Depending on how much inventory you have, costs will vary, but they can certainly run into the thousands. This model can be profitable, but you will have to spend money up front.

Amazon Keyword and Regular Research Skills - Similar to keyword research and SEO skills, you will need to know how to research keywords on Amazon. It's a similar process. You can use the Amazon search bar to type in keywords to see what comes up. Once you see a product to what you want to sell, look at your competition. You then have to figure out a way to make a different or better product with your own branding. This requires you to look up manufacturers, oftentimes, overseas manufacturers, to come up with the best price point. You also have to research shipping cost as well to get the best deals.

Negotiation skills - This business model requires you to have great negotiation skills. Every little dollar or cents you can get at a discount will help you in the long run, meaning more profit. When you're working with overseas manufacturers, as a lot of people who uses business model do, you will need to be diligent about getting the best deal that you want. However, you do not want to sacrifice quality. So be diligent with your research.

How Long Does It Take To Start - Days to Months

This business model is research and capital-intensive. To truly be successful at this model, you will have to do research. If you don't, and you skip the research step, then you will leave dollars on the table and possibly even lose money. Because you're dealing with so many inventories, you don't want to end up spending dollars they go down the drain.

What to Do to Get Started

1.   Research the products that you want to use with Amazon FBA. Find a product and look at the competition. Then ask yourself a few questions. Can you make a better product at a cheaper price? Can you make a similar product at a similar price? Then, you need to research manufacturers to see what manufacturing costs can be and how you can create a better product. During this stage, you will also want to research freight transportation costs, too, and see who is great at dealing with international shipping. Flexport is a popular one to use. You'll also need to research the best shipping options if you are in the same

country as the manufacturer, too.

2.   Once you have found a manufacturer that you think can create your product, reach out to them to see if they can make a model for you and send it to you. Then examine the prototype or model to check the quality and see if you want to order a bigger quantity or not.

3.   You'll then want to purchase a barcode for your product and then agree to the terms of the manufacturing deal.

4.   Communicate with your freight shipping company to get your wares to an Amazon warehouse.

5.   Make sure you have an Amazon Seller account so you can set up the listings for your product.

6.   Then set up your Amazon FBA account and create shipping. You also need to prepay for all your shipping labels.

7.   Ship the labels to your Freight Forwarder. Start marketing your product.

8.   Once you sell your first shipment, you can then fine-tune the process to make more profits. Do it again or you can branch two different products.

☐

9.

Pros and Cons

Pros

One major pro of this business model is the money that you can make. Because you are buying items in bulk, you have the potential to make a large amount of money. However, this can also be a con.

Cons

Because you are dealing with items in bulk, you have to make sure that your marketing is superb. You want to make sure that you can sell your goods in a timely fashion. The longer they stay, the more you are charged to keep them housed at the Amazon warehouse. You also want to make sure that your research and your budgeting is topnotch to avoid wasting money and paying more and unnecessary fees.

Another con is that you are exclusive to Amazon's website. If for any reason you get your account shut down, then you are out of luck.

Why People Fail

Amazon FBA is ripe for failure if you are a beginner. It is an easy way to sink a lot of money quickly. If you're going to do this business model, you want to make sure that you're taking your time and not rushing it. Start with a small order before you woke up to a thousand plus units. You want to make sure that you can handle a small inventory before going all out.

☐

Online Arbitrage

Intro

This business model utilizes Amazon FBA, but it allows you to source your products from online retailers instead of using an overseas manufacturer to make the products.

Skills and Monetary Investment

Research Skills - Research skills are a must for this business model. You have to find the best products that make money. Then you have to find the product cheaper on another retail website that will give you the profit that you want.

Writing Skills - You need to know how to write advertising copy and high-converting product listings on Amazon that sell.

Monetary Investment - $0- $1000+

This business model requires much more in capital, but it is more flexible in how you source your products. Some of the initial costs are signing up for an Amazon Seller's account. Once you find a product worth selling in bulk on another website, you then have the inventory sent to the Amazon facility. Once the inventory gets to the Amazon facility, you will have to pay warehouse and fulfillment cost. Amazon will charge you on your products and to ship it out for you. Depending on how much inventory you have, those costs will vary, but they can run into the thousands. This model can be profitable, but you will have to spend money up front.

Amazon Keyword and Regular Research Skills - Similar to keyword research in SEO skills, you will need to know how to research keywords on Amazon. You will also need to research coupon sites and other sites to find cheap items in bulk. You then have to research the shipping cost it would take to get these items to the Amazon Warehouse. The longer you can research to get the best deals, the more it will benefit you in the long run.

How Long Does It Take to Start – Day to Weeks

This business model is research and capital-intensive. Because you're dealing with everything online, research will be a major component if you are successful or not. Just when you think you've found everything you need, don't be afraid to research more because it can help you save a deal by finding that coupon or extra deal that can help you make more profits.

What to Do to Get Started

1.   Research the product that you want to use with Amazon FBA. Find a product and look at the competition. Then beginning looking at other online retailers like Target or Walmart to see if you can find that product cheaper in bulk.

2.   Make sure your Amazon Seller account is up so you can set up the listings for your product.

3.   Once you've found your product, ship the items to your house or designated warehouse.

4.   Then set up your Amazon FBA account and create a shipping label. Add the labels to your product once they arrive at your house. You also have the option of letting Amazon do your labels for a small fee if you don't want the inventory coming to your house first. That's up to you and how much you want to make.

5.   Send your items to Amazon FBA.

6.   Start marketing your product.

Pros and Cons

Pros

A major pro of this business model is the money that you can make. Because you are buying items in bulk, you have the potential to make a large amount of money. However, this can also be a con.

Cons

Because you are dealing with items in bulk, you have to make sure that your marketing is superb. You want to make sure that you can sell your goods in a timely fashion. The longer they stay, the more you are charged to keep them housed. Margins can be slim so if you fail to move your product fast enough it can go rapidly go from profitable to unprofitable .

Why People Fail

People fail with this model because they don't find prices cheap enough. Make sure that if you're buying from online sites, the price is at a point where you can make the profits you need to keep yourself sustainable. Another way to fail easily with this model is the shipping cost. Ordering in bulk from a lot of different sites can be expensive depending on the websites policies. Be aware and alert to the shipping cost so it does not eat your profit.

☐

Freelancing

Freelancing, or service-based online businesses, are extremely easy to start. However, one of the major things to look out for when starting this business is swapping yourself with so much work that you don't have any work-life balance. Keep that in mind as you read through these options.

Freelance Writing

The great thing about writing as a freelancer is that you are utilizing skills that you are good at. You don't have to worry about any inventory, so that is not a concern or a barrier to begin.

Skills and Monetary Investment

Writing Skills -If a freelance writing gig is what you're looking for, you need to know how to write. The great thing about this online business model is that as long as you can create content, you will always have a job.

Research Skills - If you want to be a freelance writer, you need to know where to find gigs. You can look from online marketplaces such as Upwork.com, Fiverr.com, or even iWriter to find gigs. One of the most overlooked places to find writing gigs is Craigslist. Once you get your feet wet, you will want to make more money. This is where your research skills will also come in handy. You will be able to find ways to specialize as a freelance writer and get into higher in writing gigs such as tech or medical writing. There are also lots of resources that coach you on how to become a better writer and how to make more money. Also, research skills will come in handy as you may have to write different topics that you may not be familiar with for clients.

Time Management - Time management is important to all business owners, but it is especially important for freelancers. The time you spend writing is valuable because that is how you make your money. You must know how to manage your time to optimize your salary. Using dictation tools and even discovering your own process to write faster is going to be invaluable when it's time to scale your business.

Monetary Investment - $O - $1000

The best part about this business model and the freelancing model, in general, is that you don't need any money to get started. If you have a pen and paper or even a computer which most of us have, then you'll be able to be a freelance writer. The monetary investment comes in when you want to start upgrading computers or using software that can help you become a faster writer. You can even begin to spend money on Advertising to find the clients you need if you want to start making money. But your initial costs are absolutely nothing.

How Long Does It Take To Start - Immediately – Days

The most time-intensive task outside of actually writing is finding a client to work for. Thankfully, writing jobs are everywhere. If you do not want to market yourself, you can easily find gigs by using websites such as fiverr.com or UpWork.com. These gigs are great for gaining experience. Once you have an idea of your writing process and figuring out a schedule that works best for your freelance writing, you can start searching for high paying writing jobs. If you decide to work for a site or company, make sure that you understand their pay cycle. Do you get paid as soon as you turn your work in or do you get paid after it goes through a process of checking your work? Each company is different so make sure you understand so you know how to balance your workload.

What to Do to Get Started

1.   If you want to get started immediately, you can find a gig on a freelancing site. If you have some time, you can think more about what type of freelance writer you want to be. Do you want to write for magazines and journals? Do you want to write fiction or nonfiction? You can then find your gigs accordingly. If you have more time, you can even build your own website where you can find your own clients.

2.   If you're going to find your own clients, you can set up your advertisements to find them using paid advertising or do cold emails to find clients.

3.   Once you have a client, make sure that you and your client are on the same page about your milestones.

Make sure you agree on what the scope of the project is and how the work will be delivered including what's the best file to send the work to them. Afterward, make sure your pay is delivered with you. Some people prefer to get paid if they have finished every milestone. This is something that you have to work out with the client or the company that you're working for.

Pros and Cons

Pros

The pros of this business are that it is very easy to start. You don't have to have a website or any advertising or marketing experience. You can tap into gig websites and find clients easily.

The next pro about this business is that it is easily scalable. You can add more clients or take on more work to get to the financial goal that you want.

Cons

You are going to be limited by the number of clients that you can take. You only have so many hours in the day, so you have to be wise about the time you use. This is going to be similar to all of the freelancing gigs. Once you figure out a schedule that works, you didn't have to figure out a way to optimize it.

The next con is software and technical issues. Sometimes, they are unavoidable, and sometimes, they can cause a hitch in your plan. So make sure that you save, save, and save again to make sure your work is always protected.

Why People Fail

Freelance writing can be a failure if you're not charging enough for your rate. If you sell yourself short, you won't ever make the money you need to make. Don't be afraid to know your worth and ask for a higher price. Make sure that the rate you're charging can sustain your living costs.

Graphic Design

Intro

The wonderful part about graphic designing is similar to writing. It relies on your skills and no one else. To sustain yourself, you have to have a passion for graphic designing.

Skills and Monetary Investment

Writing Skills - As a graphic designer, you still have to know how to write if you want to work for yourself. Sometimes, clients require proposals and milestones for the work you want to do for them. In order to be successful at this online business, you have to be able to articulate what you can do for a client, how long each milestone will take, and the value of why they should hire you over another freelancer.

Research Skills - If you want to get your feet wet as a graphic designer, you can start off with the gig marketplaces similar to freelance writing business. However, if you want to take your freelance design skills to another level, you will need to find higher paying clients to work for. One of the great things about graphic design is there are a lot of clients who will hire you to work remotely. So, you get the benefits of being a graphic designer that can do gigs on the side with the stability of a full-time job. If you don't want to have to worry about anyone else telling you what to do, then feel free to scrap the remote job option.

Time Management - Just like a freelance writer, you have to know how to balance your time. If you can quickly figure out hacks for you to turn over projects for your client more quickly, then you can make more money. However, you want to make sure that you have a work-life balance so you're not spending all your time working.

Software Skills - Graphic designing is such that you need to know the latest software and trends to stay up-to-date. Knowing how to use tools in Adobe family or even other tools in a cloud will be helpful for you to be a successful designer. Most people want their designs at a certain format so you must know how to use that format in order to be successful.

Marketing skills - Knowing how to market yourself and your business if you decide to do print-on-demand is very important. Don't get caught up in just the artistic part of graphic designing. You should continue to develop your business skills so you can have longevity.

Monetary Investment - $0 - $1000

If you already have the software for this type of business, then you do not need to worry about spending any money upfront. If you can start off using cheap tools in the cloud or tools that are free, you can always upgrade to more expensive software later. If you only know how to use free tools, leverage the money you make from those gigs to learn standard software and move from there.

How Long Does It Take To Start - Immediately – Days

To be a graphic designer, you have to know where to find clients. A freelance market gig is always an option that already has built-in clients. Fiber always has clients ready to pay for t-shirt designs. If you're not interested in working with people, you can always tap into the print-on-demand market. It's similar to dropshipping but you just put your designs on products. When people buy your products, then you make money. Essentially, you can start as soon as you get your first client or as soon as you make your first designs to put on a print on demand object.

What to Do to Get Started

1.   If you want to get started immediately, you can find a gig on a freelancing site. You can also research print-on-demand websites to look for items and designs that are selling. You can create a similar design and put it for sale.

2.   To take your freelancing business to the next level, you can create your own website so clients can reach to you directly. You can also cold call or cold email clients. For bigger profits, you can search for companies or nonprofits that need graphic design help. If you need to build a portfolio, you can offer to do free work for nonprofit in order to get more experience.

3.   Before you secure your client, make sure the proposal is agreed upon by you both. Complete your work and be sure to save as you go. Don't be afraid to ask for referrals as this can make finding clients easier.

Pros and Cons

Pros

Starting a graphic design business is simple. You can use the skills that you already have to find clients.

The great part about this business is you can scale it by using your graphic design skills to create print on demand items.

Cons

Understanding how to maximize your productivity is going to allow you to make more money. If you want to maximize profit, you will need to find a way to take more clients.

The next con is issues involving technology. Again, if you don't protect your work, you can lose it easily which can cause a loss and profit. If you are not familiar with industry standards, then you have to learn them.

Staying up-to-date on the latest industry trends will be a con if you don't have the money for conferences. You can easily get around this con by reading the latest graphic designing blocks to make sure you are up to date.

Why People Fail

Graphic designers can fail by not letting clients know their value up front. With the gig marketplace, many people do not understand how valuable graphic designing it. It is your job to let the client know that you're worthy of the cost you're asking for in your proposal. If they don't accept, do not be afraid to move on and find a client who will pay you what you want.

Virtual Assistant

Intro

This gig is perfect for those who love to offer administrative support and be helpful. A virtual assistant is a valuable job because everyone wishes they have more time.

Skills and Monetary Investment

Virtual assistants offer help for too busy people based on the specific skill-set that they have. Virtual assistants can help administrator from marketing needs to any other needs that you can think of. This section will just highlight a few from the most popular need that people want to hire a virtual assistant.

Writing Skills - Some people want virtual assistants to do writing for them. This writing can range from writing advertisements to creating content to sending out emails to their customers. If you know how to write but don't want to write all the time, you can potentially do virtual assisting.

Research Skills - Virtual assistants offer invaluable research skills to busy people. Sometimes, people want you to do keyword research for them or find leads for them. If you are a great researcher, you can provide this service for them.

Data Entry Skills - Data entry is another sought out skill that virtual assistants offer. For people who have eCommerce doors or even some brick-and-mortar stores, data entry is not going to go out of style. These tasks can vary, but the main gist is you enter information for clients on two spreadsheets that they can use later or any type of information where you're dealing with lots of data.

Customer Service Skills - Customer service is a great need that virtual assistants can perform. For other online businesses or even some brick-and-mortar stores, you can offer customer service, so clients do not have to deal with it. If you are good at calming down upset people or dealing with a variety of personalities in a high-pressure setting, then this may be for you.

Planning Skills - There are lots of people who need help planning vacations or handling their meetings. If you are a master planner, you can be of assistance to many people who need these services.

Email Management - There are a lot of people who hate dealing with email. You can help them get organized with their emails and set it up where they won't be bombarded with email. It's a simple skill but one that is very valuable.

Sales Skills - There are some people who need help following up with leads or even setting an appointment. If you like sales, then you can always find a gig as a virtual assistant.

Email Marketing - Email marketing is an important skill that many businesses do not tap into. If you love sending out monthly newsletters and emails to help businesses stay in touch with their clients, then this is a skill you can easily advertise and get people to pay you to do.

Social Media Management skills - There are lots of people who hate dealing with social media. If you're someone who loves social media, leverage this love and offer people social media for them. Most businesses have social media and if they don't, you can consider offering it for them. This is one skill that doesn't look like it's going out of style anytime soon.

Any skill You Can think Of - Virtual assisting is all about using your skill sets to help other people free up time. If you have a unique skill-set that you know business owners or any other professional will need, then don't be afraid to let that be one of your main offerings.

Time Management - Just with any other service gig, you have to be aware of your time. You also can't get bogged down with offering too many different services because this may be able to throw your time schedule app.

Monetary Investment - $0 - $1000

You don't need any money to start being a virtual assistant. However, it may be valuable to get some experience first working a gig website to see what types of gigs you prefer. Once you figure out what you like to help people with, then you can start developing higher priced packages to sell.

How Long Does It Take To Start - Immediately – Days

You don't need anything to get started with this. After you read this book, you can get started now. You simply find the client on a gigging website and go from there. As you figure out what types of skills you like to offer businesses, you can then create custom packages that deal with only the skills you want to deal with it.

What to Do To Get Started

1.   You'll first want to find work on upwork.com or fiverr.com. There are also companies that offer virtual assistants for other people that are looking for virtual assistants. You can reach out to those companies as well to get your first job.

2.   Once you get a sense of what it requires to be a virtual assistant, you can then start creating your own packages at a higher price. Think of offering monthly packages, but don't sell yourself too short.

3.   Setting up your website and creating a way to sell to other people is very easy if you want to take your virtual assistant business to another level. You also want to make sure that you are always marketing so you won't experience the loss of clients.

Pros and Cons

Pros

The pros of this business are that you can get started right now. You tap into the skills that you already have in order to make money.

The next pro about this business is that it is easily scalable. You can make your prices higher and create monthly packages to guarantee that your income comes in monthly.

Another great pro about this business is that you can always change up the services that you offer. You don't have to stick to one skill. If you are easily bored, you won't be bored being a virtual assistant because you can do something new.

Cons

If you don't have the right client, then you may have difficulty finding people who want to pay your higher prices. You are in competition with virtual assistants from the Philippines and India and other countries that don't mind offering lower prices. However, don't get into a price match. Make sure you are comfortable with the prices you're selling. As long as your customers see the value that you offer, they do not mind paying your prices.

The second kind of virtual assisting is not navigating the professional relationship. Sometimes, you like your clients so much that you end up doing work for free. When you start a virtual assistant contract, be sure that you and the client both agree to the terms so there won't be any confusion about what you're getting paid for.

The third con of virtual assistant which is also a pro is because we have so many services that you can offer; there is a possibility of falling into a trap of not being focused. You are focusing on so many tools that you can't really focus your marketing efforts. When you first begin, focus on one to three services, hopefully, that is interrelated, so it will be easier for you to pick up the client. Once you pick up a client that pace with those services, then you can consider expanding the services that you offer. You do not want to spread yourself too thin once you start which can cause you to fail.

Why People Fail

People can fail with virtual assisting because they start off focusing on too many skills. This can cause them to wear out and become a jack of all trades and a master of none. Take your time and start off slow before branching into other skills that you offer. Another reason people can fail being a virtual assistant is that they do not charge high enough prices. You'll be surprised, but it's true. When you charge higher prices, you get up a higher quality of client. Root out problematic customers upfront by charging higher prices.

Starting Your Own Agency

Intro

Once you get so good at either writing, virtual assistant, or graphic designing on a freelance level, you have the option of starting your own agency. The great thing about signing your own agency is you get to step back and focus on recruiting people to do freelancing for you so you can pocket more money without relying just on your skill set.

Skill and Monetary Investment

Writing Skills - To start your own agency, you'll need to have writing skills. This will come in handy when you're writing advertisements to recruit people as well as advertisements to market your business.

Research Skills - If you're going to start your own agency, you need to research the best rates. You need to find people who have quality works and rates that you can hire. Or you can decide to offer your own rate but just make sure it's in line with the market value to get the best employee.

Delegation skills - Once you have your own agency, your mindset has to shift to how to manage the business. You have to keep your employees happy as well as your clients happy. If you don't have good delegation skills, you will drive yourself crazy.

Time Management Skills - Time management

becomes more important when you have your own agency. You have to make sure that you are handling the customer and employee relationship, as well as, knowing how to continue to market the business to bring in more clients so you can pay the people that work for you.

Monetary Investment - $0 - $1000+

The monetary investment for this business model is interesting. You can put money into creating your own website, but the most money you're going to stand is hiring other people. You can choose to hire people out of your own pocket or pay them based on the profits you get from your own client. You can use a dropshipping model and pay your employees once you get paid from the client. Remember that well-paid employees are happy employees and will be difficult to get away from you.

How Long Does It Take To Start - Immediately – Months

One of the quickest ways to start an agency is to begin taking more work on and using sites like Fiverr or Upwork to get others to help you. However, doing this may be tricky because you can't verify if a person has quality work or not until you actually see it. Some people like to do a trial first and then hire them. This trial can take a while, but as you create the processes for your business, you can decide how long it will take.

What to Do to Get Started

1.	To get started, you can start expanding the offerings that you currently offer for your business.
2.	Once you do that, you can start getting employees. You can either put advertisements on Indeed, Craigslist, or even Upwork or fiverr.com to hire people.

3.   Once you start getting more clients and employees, look into a project management system such as Basecamp or Slack so you can manage everyone. When you do this you have to be patient and stay on top of your deadline so your clients and employees can be happy.

Pros and Cons

Pros

The pro about this business model is that you don't have to worry about freelancing. You can spend more time running the business and doing administrative tasks.

The second pro of this business model is that you can make more money since you're taking on more clients.

The last pro is there's going to be a great sense of accomplishment once you began managing other people and making money. It will make you feel like a true business person.

Cons

The saying is true. More money can equal more problems because handling more people are going to be more stressful. If you don't like managing people or you can't handle conflict, you may not want to consider opening your own agency.

Communication can be a con. You have to make sure that everyone is on the same page from your employees to your clients. Being clear and making sure that people understand what's going on is an important aspect of owning your own business.

The last con is potential employee salaries. Some

people just like to hire employees as independent contractors, so they don't have to worry about paying taxes or health insurance for them. However, if you want to make sure they are employed full time, you will have to consider health insurance and retirement savings and taxes which can be a substantial amount of money.

Why People Fail

People fail with running an agency because they think that running an agency is similar to being a freelancer. It is not. Do not be lulled into thinking that you can handle an agency just because you are a successful freelancer. You probably are capable of having your own agency but take your time and make sure you have processes in place before you go into taking on responsibilities in your business. Create a process for hiring people. Create a process for dealing with customers. Create a process for handling conflict about delivered work. Once you create these processes, it will be easier for you to manage everything. However, take the time to create them up front so when you're actually in the middle of business, you don't have to figure it out. Another note, do not be so committed to your processes if they don't work. Be willing to change to what fits your business. The process is going to help you when times get hectic so take your time with this step.

Influencer and Affiliate Marketing

These business models are a combination of retail and freelancing. These business models are all about creating an audience and then selling to that audience with products from other people, which are called affiliate marketing, or creating your own products to sell. Using ads is another way to monetize the audience. Popular affiliate marketing platforms are Amazon, Walmart, eBay, or ClickBank. There are lots of affiliate marketing sites to come from so you can research and find the one you want to use. To begin affiliate marketing, you simply sign up for an affiliate marketing website, browse their products, and choose to promote products that are related to your niche. Once you sign up, you will be given an affiliate link and then you put that link on your website in the articles that you have written. Any time someone clicks on the link and purchases the product through your link in the articles that you write, you will get a commission. If you do not have any products, affiliate marketing is a great way to begin monetizing your site. There are lots of different affiliate websites you can choose from in order to promote your product.

Monetizing your blog through ads is the next way to potentially monetize your site. Even if you do not have a lot of traffic just yet, some advertisers are still willing to work with you. If ad revenue is your selected revenue model, there are different ad revenues that you have to decide to use as advertisements on your website. You can choose from CPC, CTA, CPM, or ad revenue models.

• CPC means cost per click. Another name for this model is PPC or pay-per-click. Just as the name says, you get paid based on if people click on your ad or not.
• Similar to this model is CPM or cost per million or how much it costs per thousand impressions.
• CPA, the last revenue model, means cost per action, you get paid dependent upon if the people who click on the ad take a certain action or not. It could be responding to the ad with an email or phone number. It just depends.

The revenue model you choose depends on how many visitors you get to your website. Similar to signing up for an affiliate management program, you also have to sign up for an ad revenue program. There are also a lot of these networks to use on your platforms like Google AdSense. Great ad networks for beginners to check out are Propeller Ad Network and Bidvertiser. Once your site gets older and has a stable level of traffic, you may want to look into Chitika and Adbluff. Hilltop Ads is another great ad network for sites with more traffic. A middle of the road solution for beginner and more experienced niche creators would be Media.net. Read through these ideas to get a sense of the possibilities you can have when you run your own influencer and affiliate marketing business.

Blogging

The fun thing about blogging is that you get to use your freelance writing skills, but you don't have to worry about dealing with customers. Before you commit to blogging, you have to decide if you want to do a smaller blog or a niche website, which is under 20 pages or do an authority website which has many more pages. Once you figure out what type of blog you want to do, then you can figure out how to monetize a blog.

Bloggers make money by either selling products that they make themselves or selling products from other people. They can also make money from advertisement. Some people even create blogs and just sell them to others. If you go into the blog, you have to decide which way you're going to make money, too.

Skills and Monetary Investment

Writing Skills - As a blogger, it is inevitable that you know how to write. These writing skills go from knowing how to write articles to emails to advertise me.

Keyword and Research Skills - Once you decide to become a blogger, you need to do research and see what other people are blogging about. How can you be different? One of the great questions is can you write over a hundred articles on a topic that you're going to write about? Knowing keywords that people search for and knowing how to optimize SEO is another important skill of a blogger. If you want your blog to do well, you want to not skip on this step.

Email Marketing Skills - A blogger has to always be in touch with their audience and one way to do that is through email. Bloggers leverage email marketing to sell more products to their audience and to offer more value to them. Knowing the basis of email marketing is an important skill to have if you're going to be a blogger.

Monetary Investment - $0 - $50

One of the best things about blogging is you do not need money to get started. If you have no money, you can tap into websites like Hub Pages or Squidoo to create your blogs. However, if you have a few extra bucks, even $20, you'll want to purchase a domain name from namecheap.com or another popular domain registration site and pay for hosting which can cost you anywhere from five bucks a month or $10 a month to host the site yourself. Then you start writing. It's relatively cheap to start writing.

How Long Does It Take To Start - Immediately – Months

It does not take a long time to get started on your blog. What takes long when it comes with blogging is gaining an audience. That's why keyword research is so important. If you already have people looking for what you're blogging about, that will help you start to get traffic. If you want to go faster and gain traffic quicker, you may want to consider paid advertising. You can consider running a $5 ad every day to help boost your traffic. Tapping into free social media traffic is a way to get more traffic to your website.

What to Do To Get Started

1. First, you want to do keyword research to make sure that the topic of your blog will have traffic. You can also look on Amazon to see if there are any products related to your block that you can put advertisements on

your website about.

2.   You can first make an account on HubPages or Squidoo if you don't want to spend any money. If you don't mind spending a few bucks, you can register your domain name and order hosting. Then, you'll install WordPress if you're going for this option which will allow you to add articles to your site.

3.   Once you have your website up, write your articles and put them on your site.

4.   After you add your articles, consider adding links to Amazon products that are related to your website in the article or in the sidebar. Once you sign up for Amazon Affiliates or any affiliate website, they will give you the links you need to include on your site. You can add these links and pictures to your articles and sidebar of your blog.

5.   Also, make sure you have a way to capture your visitors' email so you can always market to them through email.

6.   To take your profit journey to the next level, consider making your own products to sell to your customers.

Pros and Cons

Pros

Starting a blog is easy if you're a great writer. It's all the benefits of a freelance writer without the stress of dealing with clients.

There are so many ways you can make money with a blog even if you don't have money initially. You can sign up for an affiliate website like JVZoo, ClickBank, or eJunkie, or Amazon and Walmart, and sell their products to the readers on your site.

You can write all your articles up front and then drip them over time. To drip an article means that you use software to post an article to your website automatically without you having to manually post the article. So you can initially write all of your articles upfront and then forget them by using dripping software.

Another pro about starting a blog is that you can write anything that you want. There are so many topics that you can surely be interested in what you want to write about.

Cons

Writing articles can take a long time. It can take anywhere from 50 to 70 hours upfront to create all the content for your blog. However, this does not have to be a con. If you're committed to the blog, you can write the articles and post them once a month. You can also hire people to post the content for you.

You have to be consistent. For people who lose focus easily, you may want to focus on niche sites and then scale up to authority sites.

Sometimes, gathering traffic can be slow. You have to be patient and don't throw in the towel too easily for this business model.

Why People Fail

People fail with this model because they give up too quickly, and they don't do proper research beforehand. Make sure that your keywords are ones that people want to buy. You may be interested in a topic, but it may be a topic that people are not interested in. They may also not be interested in purchasing items around the niche. Try to look for items that cost $100 or above that you can bring in enough profit from your affiliate sales.

YouTube

Creating a YouTube channel is another great online business. Similar to blogging, the topics you can start on YouTube are endless. As long as you have a computer and internet connection, then you are good to go.

Skills and Monetary Investment

Writing Skills - Just because you're YouTubing does not mean that you don't need writing skills. You still need to write great descriptions and some people like to write a script to their videos.

Keyword and Research Skills - Keyword and SEO research are going to be just as important to you as a YouTuber as it is to blogging. SEO will help people find your YouTube channel easier if your videos are SEO optimized.

Email Marketing Skills - Even though you have a YouTube page, you still want to drive your subscribers a page where you can get their email. This will ensure that if something happens to your YouTube page, you can always reach the people that subscribe to you.

Monetary Investment - $0 - $100

You don't have to have any money to start a YouTube channel. You should use the tools that you already have. If you need to buy lighting for your backdrop, that can be a small initial cost, but you can use lamps that you already have until you make more money to invest in better lighting. However, if you want to jump right into reviewing certain products, you may have to pay for the products if companies do not give you the product. As long as you are consistent, you may start getting offers to review things for your Channel.

How Long Does It Take To Start - Immediately – Days

Starting a YouTube channel can be done in a matter of hours. Create a Gmail account if you don't already have one and then go to YouTube and start your channel. You want to make sure that you're optimizing your About Page so people can find you. If you can do the research with your keywords, take your time to come up with topics that will help your site be more successful. Look at what other people are doing and see how you can add your special touch- that's an easier way to get started. YouTube is all about popping on trends, so in this case, knowing what your competitors are doing can be helpful to you.

What to Do to Get Started

1.   Before you start your YouTube channel, make sure you do keyword research and check out other YouTubers in the same niche. Create a list of topics that you want to start your YouTube channel, so you can at least create 10 videos.

2.   Start your YouTube channel. Make sure the homepage of your YouTube channel and your About Page is customized. Also, include an email so people can reach you if they want to.

3.   Once your YouTube channel is up, go ahead and make those first 10 videos. Then you can upload them and create a content schedule after that. Whether you're going to post twice a day or twice a week or twice a month, whatever your schedule is, stick to it and be consistent.

4.   Once you start getting more traffic, figure out ways to monetize your site. Are you going to do sponsorships or ad? Are you going to promote other people's products or your own product? Having something to sell can help you make money from your YouTube channel.

Pros and Cons

Pros

A YouTube channel is one of the easiest ways to get started on an online business. You do not have to worry about paying for domain names and hosting. You simply create your channel, upload a few videos, and you're off.

YouTube is an easy way to find content if you look for other people. So that's another pro to have a YouTube channel. YouTube pairs well with blogging; there's no reason why you can't do both.

Cons

One of the major cons of having a YouTube channel is that you do not own YouTube. You can have a million followers but if your channel is shut down, you lose that audience. If you're going to have a YouTube channel, it's important for you to have your own blog that you can encourage people to go to and visit you. That way, you're protected in case something happens to your YouTube channel.

YouTube changes its rules frequently. You want to make sure that you are protected in case they do that. You have to remember that just because a million people viewed your video does not mean that a million people are buying from you. Be vigilant about capturing peoples' emails so you can always have access to them and sell to them no matter what YouTube does.

Being consistent is one of the difficulties of having a YouTube channel. People lose interest, so if something comes up in your not able to post, they may think that you're not committed. Growing a channel that can generate significant income will take time, commitment and a long-term plan.

Why People Fail

People fall into the trap that lots of videos mean lots of dollars. It doesn't. If you're going to have a YouTube channel, make sure that you have another way to reach your customers. Having emails from your customers will help you to find the most engaged subscribers and they often are the ones who spend the most money. Create a viable funnel outside of YouTube that will allow you to continue to reach your subscribers outside of YouTube.

Social Media Influencer

A social media influencer is similar to being a YouTuber. Instead of using YouTube as a primary vehicle to promote other people's products or their own products, social media influencers use social media platforms such as Instagram, Facebook, Pinterest, or even Snapchat. They essentially use whatever social media platform they prefer to get an audience and sell people's products.

Skills and Monetary Investment

Marketing Skills - Social media marketers know how to market products. They are masters at creating content that captures the audience and then monetizing that audience.

Sales Skills - Whether they are passively or actively selling, social media influencers are always selling. If you're going to go this route, you must figure out the best way you feel comfortable selling.

Email Marketing Skills - It is always ideal to send people to your own personal website. That way, if something happens to the social media platform at any time, you will still have that information. If you can capture their emails, you can then leverage email marketing to always sail to this audience.

Monetary Investment - $0

If you're using social media to make money, you don't have to buy a domain name or any registration. However, if you want a backup, you can spend a few bucks in getting it on domain and hosting.

How Long Does It Take To Start – Immediately

This does not take a long time to get started. You can start as soon as you finish reading this book, but you may not be able to make any money until you start getting more people to see your information. So be patient until you can build more traffic.

What to Do to Get Started

1.   You sign up to the social media platform of your choice. You may also want to consider what type of content you're posting. If you want to target a certain group like mothers or athletes, make sure your content is for them. This focus on your content will allow you to market to other people easier.

2.   Start posting and getting an audience. Pay special attention to your content that captures the most interest. Then create more of that content.

3.   Once you start getting followers, then you can start promoting. You can either reach out to other people or you can wait for them to contact you. However, it is best to be proactive because not everyone needs a million followers. If you have some people who are interested in very specific audiences and if you can provide that for them, they will pay you to promote their information.

Pros and Cons

Pros

The best part about this model is it only takes five minutes to sign up for a social media website. You get to sign up on the site that you want and post what you want which gives you a lot of freedom.

You don't have to worry about creating your own

products. As long as you have an audience, there's somebody that will pay you to reach them. This is one model that you can always find a way to make some money from.

Cons

Just like having a YouTube channel, you do not own the social media platform. So you want to make sure that you're protecting yourself and having some type of backup in case your platform is ever shut down.

Some people require that you have a certain number of followers before they promote with you. Getting followers can take time, so if you want to have more followers quickly, you need to have to post content all the time. If you love being on social media, then this should not be an issue.

Social media can sometimes be draining so you have to protect yourself from social media fatigue. If this is the business model you choose, it's okay to take a break from social media for a few minutes a day. You don't have to be on it 24/7 in order to make money. Post sometimes to see how people react, and then go back and do it again.

Why People Fail

Similar to YouTube, people fail because they are not focused on reaching out to people outside of the social media platform. They also fail because they don't adjust their content. Yes, it's fun to post content that you like and love, but if you're going to be a social media influencer, you have to post the content that other people respond to. If you do that and can adjust quickly, then you can have success.

Congratulations! You've made it through this section full of information. I know it may feel overwhelming but take a deep breath. If your head is spinning yes, that's a good thing. It means you've taken a lot of great information in. If your head is not spinning, that's also a great thing. It means that you have a great sense of concentration. You now have all the information you need in order to be successful. You don't have to spend thousands of dollars buying courses that make the creators rich or read a lot of books. Just pick one idea and began. Once you pick your idea, you can find a free guy that will walk you through the process in more detail. Hopefully, you've highlighted some of the information that interests you the most. Keep the information that you have gathered from this chapter for the next chapter where you will be getting more insight that can help you figure out which business model to use.

CHAPTER 3: WHICH ONE? PICKING YOUR ONLINE BUSINESS MODEL

Once you consider this information, you can then focus on certain bones you must have no matter what business you choose to run, including branding, websites, and marketing strategies. This chapter will focus on the bones of your business and then ask a few other questions that you will need to decide upon before choosing your business model.

One of the important bones of your business is the brand concept. Simply put, the brand concept is about what your brand represents. To help form your brand concept, you will want to ask yourself a few important questions.

• When people see your brand, what ideas do you want them to associate with your brand? - Do you want them to think of youthfulness or maturity? Do you want them to think of free-spirited people or business-minded people? What other ideas do you want them to think about when they hear your brand's name or see your brand's imaging. There is no right or wrong answer to this. It is simply what you want your brand to be.

• What is your mission statement? - You may think a mission statement is a broad, detailed story, but it is simply what you want your company to do or be. What kind of goals do you want to reach with your company? Do you want to be the top-grossing baby line company in the world or would you like to be the most successful luggage company in the world? Do you want to help stop poverty with a portion of your sales? Whatever your goal is for your company, that is what your mission statement should be.

• What is your brand story? - Your brand story is different from your mission statement; although they may share some. The brand story talks about the origins of your company, whereas, the mission talks about the goals of your company. You can incorporate your origin story or the initial idea that inspired you to start your company. People connect to a brand story because they are able to see themselves in the brand. Make sure that the brand story is written in a way that's relatable and truthful. It is a foundational aspect of your business.

• What colors do you want to represent your brand question? - Choosing the colors of your brand is very important. If your brand has a calm vibe, then you most likely will want a calm color to represent your brand. A fiery color like orange and red may not be ideal, but a cool color like blue or light green may be more ideal. However, there is no hard-and-fast rule for the colors that you choose. Your brand makes color. Do not stress if your colors are like another business because there are only so many colors in the world, so a few businesses are bound to use the same kind. However, make sure that your colors represent your brand in a way that it is not used by another brand. That's where your brand story in your mission statement comes into play.

• What logo would you like to represent your brand? - Some people like to just use logos or initials to represent their brand. The type of font used in the logo is also part of the brand. There are lots of different companies that can help you develop your brand. A popular website to use is fiverr.com. The designers there will ask you questions, and you can brainstorm with them to find your brand for cheap. Other people like to use free logos and add their own fonts with a website like Canva, which is another low-cost option.

Once you have your initial branding down, you will then want to think about your target market. They may influence your branding efforts as well. A great activity to do when trying to figure out whom your target market is to create three brand identities of the people who will buy your product. This helps you to learn more about your customers and find a brand that will appeal to them. It is important to know multiple types of customers you are targeting because different target markets will be attracted to your business for different reasons. Knowing your target audience may help you prevent a no-no. For example, if you have a vegan company, you may not want to have a bloody cow as your logo. Thinking about your customer can help you come up with cool ideas and ways that you can connect to them. When trying to figure out who your target market is going to be, you want to do your research. You may realize that your idea may not work after you do research. However, these three brand identities will help you research further and find out more about your customer. It is important to note that when you begin, you will learn more about your customers. As the information comes in about who is buying your product, do not be afraid to adjust some of your branding efforts at the point.

When you think about the brand identities, here are a few questions that you can ask.

• Where is your customer from? What country or continent are they from? What city in that country are they from?

• How old is your target demographic? Try to narrow this down as much as possible. Have one major segment and then another major segment for two major target demographics.

• Will your business solve a certain problem for them? Is your target demographic unable to find a brand or a product that speaks directly to them. How will your brand set itself apart for your ideal customer?

• Where does your customer stay most of the time when they are on the internet? Are they browsing social media or are they on news websites?

• How do you get your promotion in front of them? Are you going to use advertisements on a search engine or social media websites?

• What are their hobbies? What do they love to do already? What hobbies are they spending money on to do?

• What do they like to read? What genres do they like to read? Do they prefer audio books, printed books, magazines, or blogs?

• What do they like to eat? Are they plant-based or love meat? Do they care about where the animals they eat come from?

• Are they healthy? Do they suffer from chronic illnesses?

• Are they married? Are they divorced? Are they in long-term relationships? Are they in homosexual or heterosexual relationships?

• Do they have children? How many? Are these children that they birthed? Are these children that they adopted? Do they have trouble conceiving?

• Are they homeowners? Or do they rent? What type of homes are they living in? Brownstones? Ranch homes?

• What type of interior décor is their style? Modern? Farmhouse? Contemporary? Chic?

• Do they travel? Do they travel domestically or internationally?

• Are they educated? If so, how much education do they have? What's the highest education they have?

• What do they do for a living? Are they blue-collar or white-collar workers?

• Do they have pets? Do they have dogs or cats? Or fish?

• What type of cars do they drive? Do they love luxury, hybrids, and practical?

• What movies do they watch? What are their favorite genres?

• What TV shows do they watch? Are they watching cable or a paid service like Netflix or Hulu?

Forming a detailed profile and multiple profiles will help you to make connections with your target market in ways that you would not have done had you not been as detailed. Be as detailed as possible and look for connections. It will help you market to them as well. The step should not be taken lightly. Take the time to sit and think through this. You can give yourself a few hours in a room with a pen and paper or with your computer to take notes. Do not have any distractions. Do not turn the TV on, and you can even turn your phone off. Having a very focused niche target demographic can be the difference between success and failure. You can mark it to more than one target demographic. However, you have to start with at least one target demographic first. Build on one target demographic, have success with that target demographic, and then move to the next target demographic. Next thing you know, you will be selling to lots of people. Just remember that you have to crawl before you walk.

Ultimately, the brand for your company is something you should not stress about because companies rebrand all the time. Starting the company with a solid brand is more important than letting your brand stop you from getting started. These three brand identities are a great place to start, and it will help you research further and find out more about your customer. If you have the money for it, you can also hire a brand consultant to do the heavy lifting for you. If you have local business accelerators in your city or an SBA office or any nonprofit that helps economic development in the city, they may have workshops for developing your brand. So be sure to take advantage of these free opportunities to get feedback about your business. Once you have a solid brand concept, it is important to move to the next step which is figuring out what type of business model is best for your online business venture.

The next important bone of your business that you want to have is your website. Your website is an important draw in bringing people to you. There are a few different ways to help bring your website to life. You also want to make sure that your website ties into your branding. If you have certain colors in your logo, you want your website to reflect those colors as well. You want to make sure that you are using a similar font on your website that's in your logo. That way, you have a consistent branding message no matter where they see an asset advertising your business.

The types of options you use for your website are depending upon your budget and your technical skill. It also depends on how much time you have and what type of tools you want to take advantage of. We will discuss a few different ways to create your website including Shopify, Big Cartel, and WordPress.

One of the most popular ways to create your business's website is to use Shopify. Shopify is highly recommended because many people already use it, and they have many great back-office tools. Shopify also easily connects to many print-on-demand services easily. Shopify has a free two-week trial that you can use, but in order to actually sell on your website, you will need to pay at least the minimum pricing to have access to the selling features. Using Shopify is a very popular option. Many successful companies use Shopify. There is a lot of support from the Shopify website itself, along with Shopify communities, blogs, and tutorials about how to use Shopify. Therefore, if you go with this option, you will not fail for a lack of information.

At this time, Shopify has three different tiers. The first year is the basic tee, and it cost $29 a month. The next tier is $79 a month, and the highest tier is $229 US dollars a month. Every Shopify tier allows you to create discount codes and sell unlimited products on your website. It also gives you a way to email people if they abandon their cart, and it protects your website from hackers with an SSL certificate. This certificate is needed to protect the credit card information of people that by your products. The higher Shopify tier you purchase, the more bells and whistles you have access to.

Shopify has a payment system built-in that they charge you to use. It is built-in so you will want to adjust your pricing to account for their processing charges. If you are using the most basic tier of Shopify anytime you make a sell, you pay 2.9% plus 30 cents if the customer is using an online credit card. If you have the first tier, and the customer is paying in person, then you only pay 2.7% of the price. If the customer is using any other payment method, there is a 2% charge. If you are using the second Shopify tier anytime you make a sell online, you pay 2.6% plus 30 cents if they are using an online credit card, but if they are using any other payment method, then there is a 1% charge. If you are using the third Shopify tier anytime you make a sell online, you pay 2.4% plus 30 cents if they are using an online credit card. If they are using an in-person credit card, they only pay 2.74%, and if they are using any other payment method, it is a 0.5% charge. With all the tiers, you have the ability to print shipping levels which makes your order fulfillment easier. Shopify is relatively easy to use, and it has a lot of bells and whistles in the backdrop. If you ever want to customize your Shopify website, you can either buy a theme or use the free themes that they have to customize your website.

If you want to buy a domain name to represent your business, you can use your Shopify store with that domain name. Shopify also has 24/7 hour support for any questions you may have which is a major perk. If you want to sell just on your social media platforms without having a Shopify website, you could consider Shopify Lite. This does not give you the option to create your own Shopify store, but it is a lot cheaper than the basic plan and it starts off at $9 a month. Depending on what country you are in determines how you will be paid. You can connect your PayPal or your bank account to Shopify. And for US customers, every two days, Shopify will put your profits into your bank account or PayPal account. You also need to be aware that the fees will be taken out of your payments before it is deposited into your account.

Anytime you are setting up an online presence to take

payments, you have to be mindful of the fees that you may be charged. Some e-commerce websites charge a fee just to use their payment processing. Payment processing is important because it is a secure way to accept payments, and you do not have to worry about setting a secure way to process money on your own which can be a strenuous process. So you have to be aware of the fees that your e-commerce processing may charge. For example, if they are using a payment processor like PayPal or Stripe, they will take a fee of the cost and the website will take the processing fee, too. These fees are minimal, but they can still add up. You should also make sure that the payment processor or the e-commerce site you are using does not have any minimum processing requirements. Some require that you make a certain amount of sales every month, or they will charge you a fee. When examining the site that you want to use to set up your business, be mindful of that. In order to make the most money, you want to make sure that you have the most options for your customer to make a payment with, too. Not everyone has PayPal, not everyone has Stripe, and not everyone has a Visa. If you have the majority of payment options, then you will be okay. You also want to think about whether you are going to accept cashier's checks or personal checks. Most payment processors are also safeguarding you against fraud, so you do not have to worry about accepting payments from fraudulent credit cards. If you wanted to find any extra designers for hire in setting up your Shopify store, there is a marketplace for you to get assistance.

It is also rather easy to connect print-on-demand websites to Shopify. After you create your Shopify store, there is a place for you to select apps to connect to your Shopify in the back office. A popular print-on-demand app to use is called Printful. To connect it, you would need to login to Shopify. Then select the Apps option. When you select the apps, you will select the Printful app and connect your store to Printful. You will be required to submit your billing information, which you should do at that time. Next, you want to make sure that the products you are selling on Printful are already listed in your Shopify store. Once your products are created, then you will go to your Printful app in your Printful account. In the back surface of Printful, you go to the store and then click on products. At this point, your Shopify products should show up in the Printful interface. You can then select the products from your Shopify store that you want to be fulfilled by Printful. You will be asked about the information and the picture of the product. Once that information is added, you are finished. Once set up, any item that is on your Shopify is now fulfilled by Printful. Other print-on-demand apps that you can use with Shopify are Printify, Teelaunch, Gooten, Pillow Profits, Print Aura, and Viralstyle. The good thing about Shopify is that new apps are being added daily that allows you to fulfill print-on-demand products. Most of these apps have a similar process to Printful that you add the app to your Shopify store. Shopify is a robust first choice option that many people choose to use, and with good reason.

Another option for a website is Big Cartel. Printful also connects to Big Cartel in the back end. Big Cartel is an e-commerce website that was made with artists and creatives in mind. Their price is not quite as expensive as Shopify. Their pricing tiers start off a little bit cheaper than Shopify. Big Cartel does have a limit on how many products you can upload to the site. Whereas Shopify has unlimited products no matter which tier you purchase, Big Cartel's first tier is free, but it only consists of 5 products. When you start selling more than five products, then you have to pay. The next level on Big Cartel of 25 products costs $9.99 a month; to sell a hundred products, it costs $19.99 a month; to sell 300 products, it costs $29.99. Big Cartel does not take a portion of your payments for processing, but they have a limited number of payment options they accept. They only accept Stripe and PayPal as payments. So you will only be responsible for the fees that PayPal and Stripe require. It is 2.75% for Stripe and 2.9% + $0.30 for PayPal. Shopify also has many integrations that you can use compared to Big Cartel. Big Cartel also has standard themes, but you can change the themes for free as well.

A quick note about domain names. A domain name is just the name of your website. You can purchase one from a domain name seller or hosting seller. A domain name is what allows your domain name to come on the internet. Sites like Big Cartel or Shopify already pay for hosting so you just point the sites to your domain name. This means that when your domain name is typed in, it will go straight to your Shopify or Big Cartel store instead of the longer name that you get when you sign up for free. Some people like to have a matching domain name with their brand without the Shopify or Big Cartel details in their domain name. For others, they want to save money so they keep the name that Shopify or Big Cartel gives them when they open their store. It is totally up to you which option you think is best. If possible, you will want to choose a '.com'. Most people view this type of website as legitimate once they visit, and it helps people to find your website easier. If there is not a domain name with the '.com' option available, other popular names include '.magazine,' '.info,' '.site', '.review', or '.co'.

When you are checking for domain names, also be aware of the renewal charge. Every time you buy a domain name, you have to renew the domain name yearly. This renewal charge allows you to maintain ownership of the domain name. If you do not pay the renewal charge, you no longer own the website. The renewal price will be listed so make sure it is a price that you can afford. Sometimes, it is cheap to buy the domain name but the renewal price can be a lot of money. You will also want to make sure the domain comes with some type of protection like 'Whoisguard' which protects your personal information. When you register your domain name without 'Whoisguard' protection, when people look up the website, they can see your personal details that you included in the purchase of the website, so you want to protect yourself if you can. Most companies include this type of protection for free and you renew it for a few bucks the following year when you renew your site.

However, if you do build a site from scratch, you have to power that website to turn it on by buying a hosting package. Web hosting allows your site to pop up in the browser when you buy the domain name. Web hosting is essentially the electricity that turns the light on in domain's house. When selecting your web hosting options, try to purchase the option that has the fastest loading times. This will ensure that your loading times are fast, and people will stay interested in the information on your site. Some hosting companies give you a free domain name once you purchase a web hosting package. Scout to make sure you get the best deal possible. You can often type in the name of the company that you are interested in using and the word discount or coupon to see what types of deals appear in the search engine results. They often cater to first-time customers and you can definitely secure a deal if you do a quick Google Search. There are certain different hosting packages that help your company handle the volume that you may receive. Popular hosting websites to visit are Bluehost, Namecheap, or even, Go Daddy. You can get a domain for less than $10 and even a hosting package for less than $5 a month.

The last important bone of your business is your marketing strategy. Once you know how much money in advertisements that you had to spend in order to get a customer, you will know how to scale easily. You want to make sure you are making note of how many followers you have month by month so you can see your growth. You can also see if the growth with your followers is corresponding to sales. Remember, marketing is all about sales. You may be doing something that is fun and enjoyable and takes a lot of time but is resulting in no sales. In that case, you may want to pivot and refocus your efforts.

Instagram, YouTube, and Facebook are three of the best sites to start marketing with initially. The first place you want to have a presence is Instagram. Instagram is important. You've got to have it. Instagram is probably the most important marketing platform for your brand in this era and one of the easiest to use. When you do start with Instagram, you can post pictures related to your business model. Making your content relevant and engaging allows others to begin to really understand what your brand does. It goes a long way towards building brand awareness. Instagram can take a lot of time, so be patient and be consistent. If anyone engages with you, make sure you comment back. Do not mind following people who say kind words or reposting people who interact with your business.

If you want to build your followers quickly, consider always running a promotion. This will keep people interested in your business. You can also consider running ads on Instagram, Facebook, or YouTube. If you can afford $2 to $5 a day, do it.

If you're not sure what type of content you can post, here are a few post ideas for your marketing efforts.

Behind the scene posts - People love to see what's going on behind the scenes. Behind the scenes posts can show what you or your employees are doing what you were doing to move the business forward like having meetings at a coffee shop. Behind the scenes posts show that you are not just a corporation, but that you are someone that has a dream and that you are going for it. You can also be funny and genuine. People can tell if you are faking or not. Let your personality show so people can relate to you.

Volunteering posts or stories - There is nothing to tug at the heartstrings and the dollar strings than by posting ways that you are involved in the community. Show that your company is not just about profits. Show how you help out in the community. People will be interested in that and be willing to support.

Cross-promotion of other brands – Cross-promotion of other brands may seem counterintuitive, but it can be a good idea. If your brand is really good for sitting in and writing in the coffee shop, why not partner with a coffee shop across the street? This way, you both are promoted, and you form a relationship with another business in the process. When you made your brand identity, you created a lot of detailed questions about what your customer likes to do. Look at that brand identity questionnaire and then try to find connections that you can use with other brands.

Celebrating popular achievements – You have milestone posts that celebrate important achievements such as reaching 100 followers, or a thousand followers, or a million followers. You can also celebrate anything in between. Just be sure to show gratitude to your follower.

Giveaways - Giveaways are a fun way to engage your followers and get more followers. When you host a giveaway, make sure you have some type of incentive for the followers, whether they are tagging other people in your posts or using hashtags, make sure that your brand is getting out.

Discounts and promotions - Make sure that if you are offering promotions that they are in line with your business. You do not want to cut into your profit so do not underprice yourself. Some businesses do not offer discounts or promotions at all, and that's okay. You have to determine if you want to offer them or not. Just do not underprice your brand if you do
.

Quotes - Inspirational quotes are always a fun way to engage your followers and to get people to follow you. Think about quotes that describe your business or the aesthetic of your business and you can use them.

Whether you're posting on social media, take advantage of hashtags so people are able to follow you easily. Use hashtags that your followers are using and make sure you have your business-branded hashtag in all your posts. This is just a hashtag specific to your posts. Try to encourage your followers to share your content so you can get more information out about your business. You can also share other simple actions to do. That way, your marketing efforts will be compounded instead of just posting pretty pictures with no actions given. Some action words that are good to have in captions are…

- Use our hashtag
- Tell a friend
- Tag a friend
- Tell us what you think
- Enter a giveaway.

Be observant and watch how other businesses are using their captions and hashtags, and do not be afraid to take inspiration from that. You also have to decide if you want to buy followers or not. Most social media platforms have policies that are against buying followers, but many people do it anyway as a way to show that people are interested in their brand. If you do purchase such a service, you will want to erase the fake followers once you start getting real followers. Nothing will kill your credibility like people knowing that you buy your followers. Try to maintain the integrity and build your brand the hard way. This will pay off better in the long run.

You also want to incorporate some form of email marketing. Ask for customer's emails in exchange for a discount coupon or a special gift if they sign up. That way, when they sign up, you always have a way to tell people about your brand. Popular email marketing systems include MailChimp, which is free up to 2,000 people, and AWeber which has a month-long free trial. An email list is very important. In case Instagram was to ever shut down your account, you will still have the emails of people who are your followers and you do not have to start from scratch. It is also important to have your own website, that way if Instagram shut you down, you still have property where people engage with your brand. When you are running promotions on your social media, be sure that some of those promotions have incentives for people who give you their email. Another great and easy way to get people's emails is when you are launching your website. You can have a countdown timer on your website and a place for them to give you your email when it launches. Having email is also important because you can send them reminder emails in case they were going to buy something from you but forgot. Shopify has this feature build in already.

There are a few other tips to keep in mind when marketing. You can have birthday promotions to reward people for being loyal to you. You can give them small gifts, coupons, or discounts. This goes a long way into building your brand awareness. You will also want to have a launch party. You can take footage of it and invite people. You can also send out press releases so people know to come. And after you launch, remember to keep marketing. Do a little bit every day so you are not overwhelmed. Just because your business is online does not mean that you are free from marketing. You still have to do it so you can have a steady stream of customers coming in. This should be one of the actions you do every day so your customers don't dry up.

Now that you know what business models you can choose from, there are a few other considerations you want to keep in mind before you decide. Running a business is not all about money. These considerations will give you other factors to think about before you start your business.

The first thing you want to keep in mind is your exit strategy. Every business has an exit strategy which means how the business is going to end. Your business' exit strategy could be to sell the business, hire other people to run the business for you, or keep running yourself. At some point, you may get tired of running your business so it's good to know how it can go on without you before you even begin. Knowing what you want to do with your business before you even begin can help you decide what type of business model you're going to choose.

The next thing you want to consider before running your business is how other people can run it for you. A lot of people fail in their business because they try to do everything themselves. This helps them to wear themselves out easier. If you can think of how your business can run without you before you begin, this will help you survive your business long-term. One important aspect of running your business is to have processes. These processes help your business function and if you are clear about that, it is easy to explain to other people. Popular processes that you want to keep in mind include customer service procedures, marketing procedures, sales procedures, bookkeeping, and social media management procedures to name a few. If you can get started with these procedures, then you will be on the right track.

How passionate you are is the next consideration you want to choose when you start your business. Some people choose their business based on how much money they're going to make. And there is nothing wrong with that. However, money isn't everything, considering how passionate you are versus how much money you are going to make it is something that only yourself can answer before you select which business you are going to start.

How much time you have now versus how much money you have is another important item to consider before you select your business. If you don't have a lot of money, but you have a lot of time, you may want to choose a business that can succeed if you have a lot of time on your hands. If you don't have a lot of money, then a capital-intensive business is not going to be in your favor, and that's okay. You can use the proceeds you make from your business to then create another business. However, start with the resources that you have now and move on from there.

The next concept you want to consider is how much time for family and other activities in your life you need. A single person has much more time to devote to their business versus somebody who has a family. Having your own business is all about being well-rounded. You don't want to be chained in your office all day with no free time. Make sure that the business model that you choose allows you to have some type of free time where you don't send the freedom that you could potentially have trying to make more money. Don't fall into the burnout trap.

Asking these questions up front can save you a lot of pain and heartache in the long run. Do the work upfront so you can be successful when things get tough with your business.

CHAPTER 4: MEASURING YOUR BUSINESS' SUCCESS

Once you have figured out what type of business model you want to follow you now have to think about what's going to make you successful. This stems back to your reason for wanting your online business in the first place. Are you tired of the nine-to-five? Are you looking for financial freedom? Are you looking for a career that's location-independent? Whatever the reason for wanting to start an online business is, think about what will make you successful dependent upon that reason. This is known as your why. Knowing why you want to do this is going to be a central component to making sure that you survive this business journey.

To help you reach your success faster. I want to go over a few concepts that could hinder you from taking action. If you're aware of these hindrances, when it happens to you, you won't be fooled by them. The first hindrance is you don't want to take action because you're afraid of failure. Yes, you're taking action by reading this book, but it does not end here. Do not be afraid to take action, and do not be afraid of failure. I'm here to tell you today that failure is a part of the business process. Business owners fail a lot, but it's not the failure that's important. It's the information they learn from the failure that helps them to make adjustments to their business quickly. That's why it's so important to begin as soon as you know what you want. This ensures that you can gather information quickly, and it is that information that helps your business be successful. If you're running an ad and you don't get any responses on it, don't be afraid to try a different ad. As soon as you know something isn't working, try something else. Using this simple concept of learning from failures quickly will help your business survive long-term.

Not just being afraid of failure, but a lot of people is afraid of not being perfect. For some reason, people expect to be perfect the first time they do something. Remember that perfection is the enemy of progress. In the business sense, it's a lot better to be adequate at something than perfect. Expect that you are not going to be perfect at first. Having unrealistic expectations has stopped many people from taking the leap into owning their own business. Do not be like these people.

So what happens when you take action and begin to make money? You need to scale your business. You scale your business by putting more money into what's working. If you have an ad that successful, put more money into that ad so you can make more money. If you have a product that sells really well, now is the time to buy more of that product to sell. If you notice that anything is bringing you in more profits, now is the time to put more money to bring even more profit.

Now that you have a steady cashflow, you will also want to consider outsourcing tasks that are not making you a lot of money. Some entrepreneurs spend so much time doing everything that they are not focusing on the tasks that bring in the most money. In this case, you will want to hire a virtual assistant to take care of tasks that you do not have time for or tasks that you do not enjoy doing. Fiverr is an excellent place to find low-cost virtual assistance. You can also Google virtual assistants from the Philippines or India for a low-cost virtual assistant that can help you with what you want to do. When you have located a virtual assistant that you may want to work with, you want to communicate with them to see how you guys communicate. Then you will give them an initial task to see how they handle it. Once they handle according to your liking and you hire them for a book or hours, you can use an app like Slack or WhatsApp to communicate with them and make sure they are helping you with what you need. A virtual assistant will free up a lot of time for you. That way, you can spend your time on more important things like making designs for your business, sending emails, and working on advertisements. Overall, be smart and grow your business. Take action, learn, and scale quickly.

CHAPTER 5: IMPORTANT THINGS TO KNOW

When you are in the initial phase of starting your business, you want to make sure that you have all the necessary business paperwork that you need so you will not be subjected to any financial trouble once your business becomes successful. This chapter will walk you through selecting your business name, getting your seller's permit, a wholesale license, and the easiest way to form your business when you are first beginning. These steps are going to require you to use your research skills. You will have to find some information on your own. It may be difficult, especially if you have not done it before. However, the good thing is that these steps are free and there are a lot of resources you will be given in this chapter that can help you should you run into any trouble. Let's begin.

The first thing you want to determine before you begin is what your name will be. You can use any type of method to come up with your name. Some people like to use their initials. Others use family names or names that have significance from important events in their life. Have fun! This is your business. However, keep in mind that your name can be a hindrance to people who will want to invest in your business. You want to make sure that the name is professional and attractive enough that lenders will not mind lending to you if necessary. You also do not want to have a profane or offensive name that can prevent you from making sales further along the line. Ultimately, you can take whatever route you want, but keeping the professionalism in a business name is advised. Once you have your name, you want to make sure that it is not trademarked by anyone else. The first thing you can do is to do a simple Google search of the name to see what pops up. You can also check your state's Secretary of State Office to check for names of businesses in your state. To do so, Google 'Secretary of State business name search' and the name of your state. You can put your business name in the search bar and see if anything pops up. Then you will want to see if your name is already trademarked. You can visit the United States Patent and Trademark Office and do a quick search there. If there is another business with your name, do not fret. You still may be able to use the name. As long as there is no other business name trademarked in your state with the same name, you are free to use the name. If you are concerned about your business's name and want to have all the protection you can get, you may consider trademarking your business' name. It is an additional cost. It is not necessary in starting out, but some people like to have that protection. Oftentimes, people like to get started with the least amount necessary and then upgrade as their business makes more money.

After you get your business name, you want to figure out how to structure your business. Small businesses are, oftentimes, structured differently from larger businesses. However, at any time, you can always restructure your business. So do not feel pressured to have it one way. Oftentimes, businesses change, so go ahead and get comfortable with constant changes. When deciding how to structure your business, you will want to consider if you want to get started doing business as soon as possible or wait a little bit later to have everything structured a certain way before you begin. The easiest way to structure your business is by setting it up as a sole proprietorship. The sole proprietorship is technically not a legal entity. A sole proprietorship just means that the person who owns the business is responsible for its debt. A sole proprietor uses their own social security number as the business tax ID. A tax ID is important because it helps the government know who to contact about getting taxes when you make money. When you set your business up as a sole proprietorship, if something happens, like someone gets injured because of your product or advice and they sue you, you will be responsible for battling the issue in court. Using your own social security for your business means that if your business suffers any financial setback and the business cannot pay from its profits, you will have to use your personal money to pay for the debt.

Some people do not feel comfortable using their own

social security number to operate their business, so they use a different method. This method is similar to structuring their business as sole proprietorship, but they just create a new tax ID for the business. The new tax ID is called an EIN. The EIN stands for Employer Identification Number (EIN) or the Federal Tax Identification Number. It is entirely free to procure. It can take a few weeks, anywhere from 4 to 5 weeks, to get your EIN number. Once you get your EIN number, if this is the option you want to take, then you are able to apply for a seller's permit or a wholesale license. When you have your EIN number, you can still operate your business as a sole proprietor, but instead of using your social security number, the business's tax ID will be the EIN number instead. The EIN number also gives you certain advantages that you can use when operating your business that a social security number does not. For example, if you have your EIN number, you are able to hire employees. You are also able to protect yourself from identity theft better. Some people like to structure their business as a sole proprietor because of ease of use. You can apply for your EIN, receive it, and be good to go. If you are going to run everything on your own in your business, this may be the easiest way to get started.

However, another popular way that people like to use to structure their business is by creating an LLC. LLC means a limited liability company. They like the extra protection that an LLC provides. If you have an LLC, and your business is sued or falls into financial difficulty, you are not obligated to pay the debts from your personal assets. You are also protected from being sued for anything as your business would be responsible, not you, the sole proprietor. An LLC can be created online, using sites like Legal Zoom, and it can be created in any state that you would like to give your business better protections. No matter how you structure your business, many people like to use their home address as the place to set up their business. However, this isn't ideal because your information will be made known in public and random people or debt collectors will have access to your information. Identity theft is real so you want to make sure that you are taking the proper precautions. There is nothing worse than thinking that it will not happen to you and it does. Prevent this from happening. Protect your information.

When setting up your business, you may want to consider using a PO Box at your local post office, which is a small yearly fee, or using a virtual office, also a small monthly fee, that allows you to use a different address than your regular address. Some people even rent a different house in order to use the house's address, but needless to say, that is an expensive option. Using a PO Box or virtual office is also helpful if you are trying to create your LLC in a different state. They just get the virtual office in the state that they want to create the LLC in and use the virtual address on the LLCs application. Certain states have better tax benefits for business and are popular to create an LLC in the state.

The top three states at the time of writing are Nevada, Wyoming, or Delaware. These places are typically more business-friendly and have limited income taxes. Delaware is popular because they do not tax out-of-state income. This means that if your business makes money outside of Delaware, you won't be taxed for it. Nevada is another popular destination to create an LLC because they do not tax business income, and they have a high level and anonymity in case the feds were ever to ask questions about your business. Wyoming is another popular place because they do not tax business income as well, and they have a higher level of anonymity than Nevada does. If you wanted to set up your LLC in one of these places, you could. It will be more expensive than a sole proprietorship. Also, the rules for LLCs change constantly depending on the state, so you would be responsible for staying up-to-date on the state's rules. You would just research their rules on the states IRS or Secretary of State's office online. Some people like to start off as a sole proprietorship, and as they make more money, create the LLC. Some LLC's require that you pay a yearly fee. You would have to research to see what applies for that state. Popular places to format your LLC is only by doing it yourself if you feel comfortable finding all the information. Other people like to visit a lawyer's office and get their assistance. This may be expensive, but there are some lawyers that can help you for free if you visit your city's local Chamber of Commerce. They would be able to help you find lawyers who can help you pro bono. Other business structures are an S-Corp or C-Corp, but these types of business structures are reserved for extremely large companies.

If you ever wanted to start the business with a friend, you can set it up as a partnership, which is similar to a sole proprietorship, but it is two or more people. You can get the EIN for the business or you can even set it up as an LLC. You want to set up your business properly from the beginning to avoid headaches later on. If you have the funds, you can probably set up as an LLC, but the ease of entry is going to be with the sole proprietorship or a partnership. At the very minimum, try to have an EIN number for your business, because of the added protection, and it is free.

There are also a few more differences you will want to consider when deciding to register your business as a sole proprietorship or an LLC. They are as follows:

• A sole proprietorship is cheaper to begin than an LLC. You do have to register the LLC in the state that your business is located in. You may have to pay annual LLC filing fees depending on the state. An LLC also has to follow the state's bylaws pertaining to LLC conduct.

• An LLC requires that your business finances and business records are separate from your personal finances and records. This means that you have to have a separate banking account for your LLC. This requirement is not necessary for a sole proprietorship but is also advised that you have a separate business account. That way, you can keep your finances separate.

• An LLC required that you have a registered agent. A registered agent has to live in the state that you are registering your LLC in, and they are responsible for being able to receive all communications regarding your business. Some people like to use a registered agent company for this.

• When you have a sole proprietorship, you are tax as a self-employed person. Whereas, when you have an LLC, you can be taxed as a sole proprietor, partnership, or corporation.

When trying to decide how to register your business, you can also consult a lawyer or accountant for further questions. To save costs, try to visit a local law clinic at a university where you can get advice from local law students. They are a valuable resource to use when you are trying to find out legal questions for your business. You can also check out nonprofits in the area to see if they have pro bono lawyers that are willing to do work. There is lots of free legal advice everywhere you go. You just have to find it.

After you have your business structure, you can then apply for a sellers' permit. The seller's permit is important to have because it allows you to sell goods and products as a business. The seller's permit also allows you to collect sales tax for the products that you sell. It is important for you to collect sales tax because you have to pay those taxes quarterly to your state government. Lucky for you, a seller's permit is relatively easy to obtain. The place to obtain the seller's permit is going to vary state by state. The seller's permit may even vary city by city if you live in a very large state. How much sales tax you need to collect will also vary state by state. The easiest way to find where you need to get a seller's permit is to Google your city's name and seller's permit. Usually, the first link that opens is going to be the officer that you can go to and purchase your seller's permit.

Most sellers' permits come as a temporary permit for selling at temporary events, like flea markets or fairs or pop-ups, or you can get a permanent seller's permit. If you want to make this a long-term business, make sure that you are filling out the application for a long-term seller's permit. Once you get the seller's permit printed off, fill it out. You can either return the seller's permit form by mail or in person. Make sure that you fill out all the information as correctly as possible to avoid any delays in getting your application processed. Another way to find the place where to get your seller's permit is to Google your state's name and 'Board of Equalization.' This will have the different regions of your state and the locations where to get your sales permit. It is important to know where to find their information because they can help you figure out where to find your local agency that can assist further. If you run into any issues, feel free to call the numbers or email them with any questions that you may have. The information they give you is free, and it is funded by taxpayers' dollars already so do not be shy to ask them. The service is already paid for. Another great resource for helping you find any permits you need will be business.gov. This is a federal website that promotes small businesses in the country. They have other great resources for you to use. As a quick note, how long it takes to get your seller's permit can vary state by state so if you are in a rush, be sure to ask your local agency the processing time so you can make sure that you have everything in place before you begin selling. It is advisable that you do not start selling until you have your sales permit. That way, you will not have to worry about any issues regarding your taxes. As another aside, you will also want to make sure that you have your sales taxes in order, too, if you are selling items online. You may even be responsible for sales tax on your website dependent on the state where the other person is buying from. When you are applying for your seller's permit, be sure to have the proper rates for sales and use taxes for your state. The attendants at the local agency will be able to help you. This information varies state-by-state, so make sure you have the right information for your state. Do not be afraid to ask questions! That will be the best way to make sure that all your questions are being answered and an easy way to navigate the process. It may feel overwhelming, but you can do it!

After you get your seller's permit, you may also need to get your wholesale license. This permit allows you to buy directly from distributors and manufacturers without having to pay retail sales tax so you can resell their products. By buying at a lower rate from a manufacturer or distributor, you will be able to make your price higher and make more profit. However, most of these businesses will not sell to you if you do not have a wholesale license. Depending on your state, the Board of Equalization may combine the seller's permit and the wholesale license so be sure to ask them if you need to get a separate wholesale license when you are applying for your seller's permit. Again, research, research, research. It is integral to find the right information.

As a heads up, this will be one of the longest, and

potentially, most difficult aspects of starting your business. However, if you are able to overcome this obstacle, it shows that you have what it takes to own your business. There is a lot of information out there about these types of services, so take your time when trying to find out the information to make sure that is accurate. It is best to get started on these steps as soon as possible, so while you are waiting for your necessary documents, you can begin working on other aspects of your business.

Another important part of a business that is crucial is how to handle your bookkeeping. One of the first things you need to do when you have a business is to create a separate banking account. This is a simple step, but many people don't have. If you combine your personal expenses with your business expenses in one account, it will be difficult to differentiate then when it comes time to do your businesses bookkeeping.

The next way to handle your bookkeeping is to decide if you want to hire somebody or keep up with your expenses yourself with software like QuickBooks. Sometimes, business resources like your SBA can offer bookkeeping help or even bookkeeping at a discount. Don't be afraid to reach out to these resources for help. Another important information you will need to keep for your business include payroll expenses and keeping up with your tax obligations. With your tax obligations, you'll also want to be sure to keep up with your tax deductions that you can possibly claim.

As a business owner, keep all your receipts for tax purposes. If you are going out to eat and discuss business, keep the receipt. Buying equipment for your business is another business expense. Services costs that you pay freelancers are also business expenses and can be used as a tax write-off. Other expenses you need to keep records of include electricity and the internet, especially if you are working from a home office. Keep track of your cell phone bill or any expenses related to your business. Have the receipts and make sure you talk to your accountant. Having a good accountant is also ideal because if you are making over $10,000 every quarter, you will need to pay taxes. When you speak to your accountant, they will let you know the best way to make those payments. It sucks for you to have a lot of money, but then have to give that money up because of taxes. Stay on top of your tax obligations.

You also want to consider ways that you can save your money. Just because you have your own business does not mean that you can save your money. Your account will be able to position the best ways for you to save money and what accounts you can use as a self-employed person. One of the most popular ways to save money is to use a solo 401(K). This type of savings plan allows you to save up to $50,000 a year. You will also want to try to look into affordable medical costs. You can check out the Freelancers Union for some of the best medical insurance policies for self-employed people and business owners.

Overall, be smart and grow your business. Your online business is able to succeed as long as you put the work into it. As you start to turn a profit, you can even craft your life to make sure that you are not letting your business consume you. Yes, you can have a business. Yes, you can have fun doing it; yes you can live your dreams. A business needs constant investment like a tree needs constant water. You have all the tools you need. Now get to watering!

CONCLUSION

Thank you for making it through to the end of Start an Online Business: A No-Nonsense, No Hype How-To Guide to Help you Pick your Online Business Model and Get Started Making Money Online. Let's hope it was informative and able to provide you with all of the tools you need to achieve your goals whatever they may be. We can't thank you enough for reading all the way through. We hope you now know what business is right for you and have already gotten started on your way to making your dreams a reality.

Chapter 1 explained the mindset you need to have in order to survive to be a business owner. All the online business models you can choose from were found in **Chapter 2**. Important considerations you need to think about along with your business model were given in **Chapter 3**. How to measure your success and scale your business was discussed in **Chapter 4**. Lastly, important information about setting up your business for long-term success was given in **Chapter 5**.

No matter what your ultimate financial goal is, you can

achieve it by starting an online business. The more online business you create, the easier the process becomes. The easier it becomes the more businesses you can start and the more money you can make in the long-run. Now, the ball is in your court. You can start with one of the easiest steps which are to get your EIN number which can be done in a matter of minutes. Then take the next easiest step and then the next easiest step. Just take action. Do not suffer from analysis paralysis. An action is the key to making your business work. There is only so much research you can do before diving in and start learning from experience.

Jim Rohn once said, "Time is more valuable than money. You can get more money, but you cannot get more time." This book has outlined everything you needed to know to get started with your online business. Do not waste any more time. Just think. If you start today, that can be a difference between you making a profit a year from now versus still waiting for the perfect time to start. Do not be a thumb-twiddler. Get to work!

Finally, if you found this book useful in any way, a review on Amazon is always appreciated!